KB244179

King Arthur

Happy House

About Wise & Wide

- A systematic 6-level English reading program based on Lexile® measures
- Diverse and interesting topics chosen from the elementary curriculums of Korea and English speaking western countries
- Well-written books in various forms including fiction stories, descriptive texts, and classics retold
- The informative but original fiction stories grab your interest, leading to the easy and clear understanding of the educational content.
- Improve thinking skills with solid after-reading activities at all levels of the series.

Wise & Wide is a 6-level English reading program that consists of 60 books and each level is systematically divided by Lexile® measures. The Lexile® Framework for Reading is the most popular reading measuring system in American formal education curriculums and many English programs. Over 20 out of 50 states in the U.S. mark Lexile® measures directly on students' final report cards and over 300 well-known publishers adopt and use Lexile® measures.

Experience many kinds of readings written by professional writers from the U.S. and England. They used interesting topics that were carefully chosen after analyzing elementary curriculums from around the world including Korea, the U.S., England, and Australia among many others. Comprehensive after-reading activities including graphic organizers, speaking tasks, and After-reading Tests are ready for you.

Levels in the series and their corresponding Lexile® measures

Level	Lexile® measures	U.S. Grade
Level 1	Below 200L	Pre K - K
Level 2	190L - 400L	Lower Grade 1
Level 3	350L - 530L	Upper Grade 1
Level 4	420L - 650L	Grade 2
Level 5	520L - 940L	Grade 3 - 4
Level 6	830L - 1070L	Grade 5 - 6

* Smart Readers: Wise & Wide level 1 is applicable to the preschool level in the U.S.

* The source of the relationship between Lexile® measures and U.S. school grades: CCSS(Common Core State Standards) FOR ENGLISH LANGUAGE ARTS, APPENDIX A (2012, which is used by 45 states in the U.S.)

Topic List

	Level 1	Level 2	Level 3	Level 4	Level 5	Level 6
Book 1	Science>Biology: The hibernation of animals Story	Science>Biology: Living and nonliving things Story	Science>Biology> Animals & the Environment: Sea otters Story	Environment> Living with nature: The diver & the persimmon tree Story	Science>Biology> Animal: Amazing animals of the Amazon Story	Science>Biology: Germs, transmitted diseases Story
Book 2	Literature> World classics: Aesop's fables Story	Literature> Traditional fairy tale: Old tales about stones Story	Social Studies> Economy: To run a business to make and save money Story	Science>Biology> Plants: Photosynthesis Story	Science>Earth science: Earth's layers,earthquakes, volcanoes, and earth's atmosphere Report	Mathematics> Sequence: The golden ratio & the Fibonacci sequence Story
Book 3	Science>Physics: How shadows are formed Story	Literature> World classics: Peter Pan Story	Science>Scientific technology: Nanobots Story	Literature>Myths: World's creation stories Story	Literature> Legend: The story of King Arthur Story	
Book 4	Literature> Traditional literature: The Talmud Story	Science>Biology> Animal: Polar bears Story	Science>Biology> Animal: Mountain gorillas Story	Social Studies> Cultural anthropology: Amazing ancient cultures of the world Story	Science> Earth science: Clouds and weather Story	
Book 5			Social Studies> Cultural anthropology: Astonishing festivals Report	Art>Music: Stories from two operas Story		
Book 6				Social Studies> People: Three great people who overcame hardships Story		
Book 7						
Book 8						
Book 9						
Book 10						

* 10 books in each level will be published.

How to Use This Book

•Before Reading

You can easily find the topic and what kind of story you are about to read.

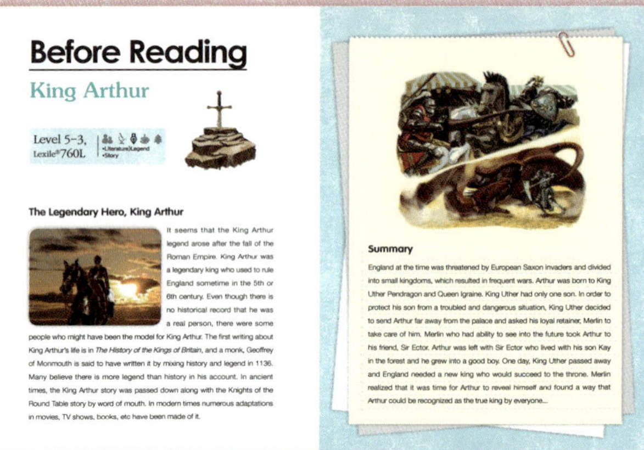

•The text

All the stories were written by professional writers from the U.S. and England, so you will read authentic and appropriate English sentences and expressions in every book in the series.

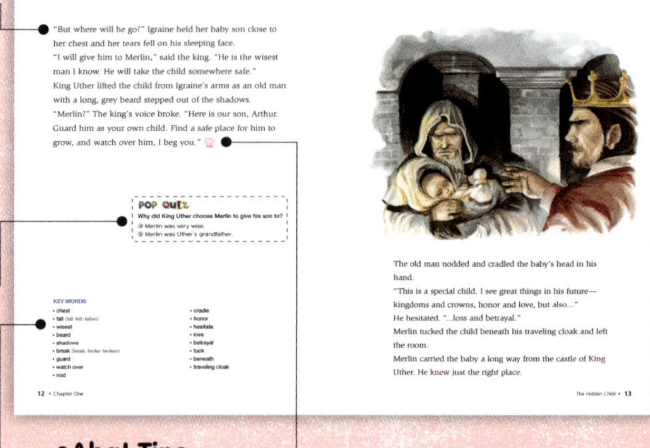

•Pop Quiz

Check out right away if you understand what you have just read by solving a pop quiz that checks your comprehension.

•Key Words

The key words and expressions on each page are listed for you to easily study them.

•Aha! Tips

Download free Korean explanations at *www.ihappyhouse.co.kr* for all of the sentences marked with "Aha!". These explain cultural, scientific, and economic knowledge or they deal with aspects of English such as grammatical structures or idiomatic expressions. There are lots of "Aha! Tips" to help you understand the text.

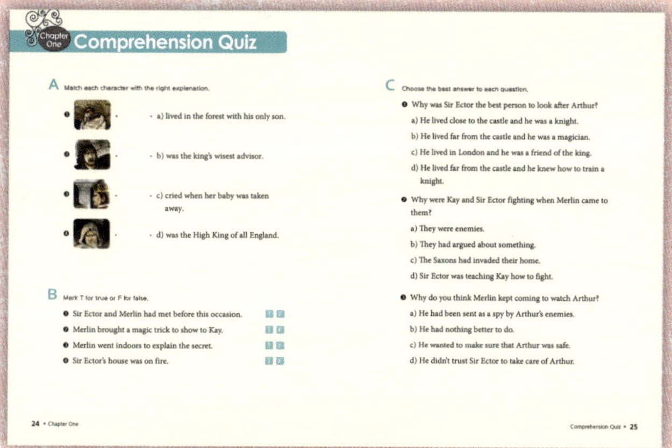

•Comprehension Quiz

After reading one chapter, solve various questions to find out if you fully understand the content.

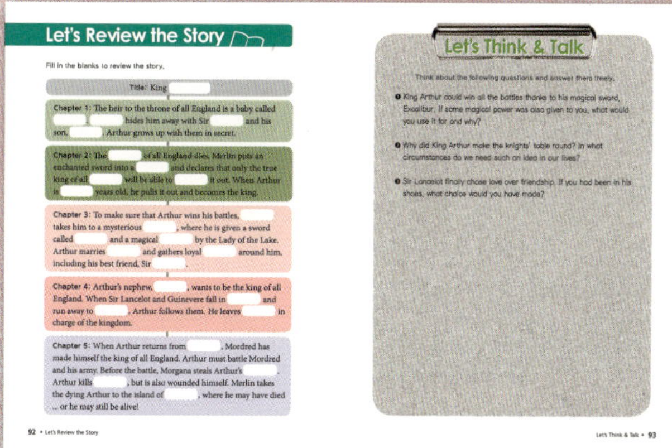

•Let's Review the Story /
•Let's Think & Talk

Fill in the blanks in the organizer to summarize the whole story. Express your own thinking and feelings about the story by answering the questions. You can build up logic and reasoning skills for your essay examinations in the future.

Appendix

Audio CD

In the CD audio book form, the texts are read vividly by American professional voice actors.

After-reading Test

Solve an additionally provided After-reading Test for each book.

The Korean translation, Answer Keys, a Word Quiz, a Word List, and Aha! Tips for each book

You can download them for free at *www.ihappyhouse.co.kr*

Before Reading

King Arthur

The Legendary Hero, King Arthur

It seems that the King Arthur legend arose after the fall of the Roman Empire. King Arthur was a legendary king who used to rule England sometime in the 5th or 6th century. Even though there is no historical record that he was a real person, there were some people who might have been the model for King Arthur. The first writing about King Arthur's life is in *The History of the Kings of Britain*, and a monk, Geoffrey of Monmouth is said to have written it by mixing history and legend in 1136. Many believe there is more legend than history in his account. In ancient times, the King Arthur story was passed down along with the Knights of the Round Table story by word of mouth. In modern times numerous adaptations in movies, TV shows, books, etc have been made of it.

Summary

England at the time was threatened by European Saxon invaders and divided into small kingdoms, which resulted in frequent wars. Arthur was born to King Uther Pendragon and Queen Igraine. King Uther had only one son. In order to protect his son from a troubled and dangerous situation, King Uther decided to send Arthur far away from the palace and asked his loyal retainer, Merlin to take care of him. Merlin who had ability to see into the future took Arthur to his friend, Sir Ector. Arthur was left with Sir Ector who lived with his son Kay in the forest and he grew into a good boy. One day, King Uther passed away and England needed a new king who would succeed to the throne. Merlin realized that it was time for Arthur to reveal himself and found a way that Arthur could be recognized as the true king by everyone...

Contents

King Arthur

King Arthur

Chapter One

The Hidden Child

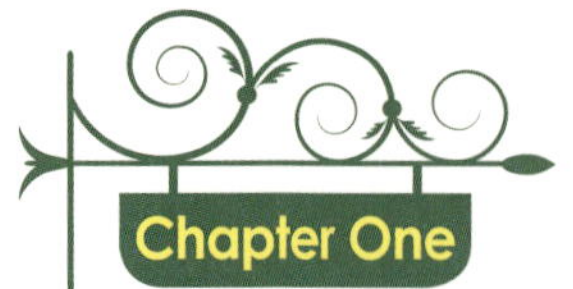

"Please, let me keep the child," begged Igraine.

Her husband, the great king and warrior Uther Pendragon, knelt before her and took her hand in his.

"My love, you know that England is a wild and dangerous place," he said.

That much was true—the land was divided into small kingdoms, and sometimes the kings fought each other. But Uther was the High King over them all.

At other times, the Saxon invaders came from Europe. Blond haired and brutal, they tried to take England as their own.

"The Saxons may attack us at any moment," went on King Uther. "It is simply not safe to keep our son, Arthur, here with us."

"But he's my baby!" sobbed Igraine. "His place is here with me."

"His place is on my throne, when I am gone," said King Uther. "We cannot risk his life since one day he will be the king."

KEY WORDS

- hidden
- keep
- beg
- warrior
- kneel (kneel-knelt-knelt)
- that much
- be divided into
- kingdom

- fight (fight-fought-fought)
- each other
- at other times
- the Saxon
- invader
- brutal
- attack
- at any moment

- go on (go-went-gone)
- simply
- sob
- throne
- risk
- since

"But where will he go?" Igraine held her baby son close to her chest and her tears fell on his sleeping face.

"I will give him to Merlin," said the king. "He is the wisest man I know. He will take the child somewhere safe."

King Uther lifted the child from Igraine's arms as an old man with a long, grey beard stepped out of the shadows.

"Merlin?" The king's voice broke. "Here is our son, Arthur. Guard him as your own child. Find a safe place for him to grow, and watch over him, I beg you." 

POP QUIZ

Why did King Uther choose Merlin to give his son to?

ⓐ Merlin was very wise.
ⓑ Merlin was Uther's grandfather.

KEY WORDS

- chest
- fall (fall-fell-fallen)
- wisest
- beard
- shadows
- break (break-broke-broken)
- guard
- watch over
- nod

- cradle
- honor
- hesitate
- loss
- betrayal
- tuck
- beneath
- traveling cloak

The old man nodded and cradled the baby's head in his hand.

"This is a special child. I see great things in his future—kingdoms and crowns, honor and love, but also..."

He hesitated. "...loss and betrayal."

Merlin tucked the child beneath his traveling cloak and left the room.

Merlin carried the baby a long way from the castle of King Uther. He knew just the right place.

After three days of walking through the fields and forests,
Merlin arrived at the home of Sir Ector.

"Sir Ector, my old friend!" called Merlin as he stepped out of
the trees into a clearing.

There was a house there, built of stone, and another low
building that smelled of animals.

A man and a boy stood facing each other, each with a sword
in his hand. The man was teaching the boy how to handle a
sword.

When Merlin called, they both turned and smiled.

"Put your sword away, Kay," said the man.

The boy, Kay, put his sword into the leather scabbard that

hung on his belt.

"Merlin!" he cried. "What have you brought me this time?

Some magic trick? Or a wounded animal to care for?"

He looked curiously at the bundle in Merlin's arms.

"Hush." Merlin pressed a finger to his lips. "It is a great

secret, and we must not speak of it here."

"Then let us go indoors," said Sir Ector.

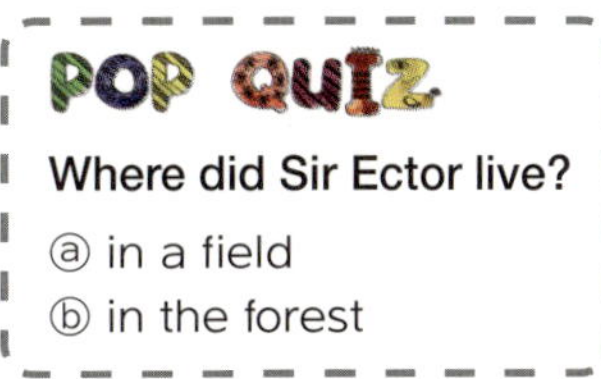

KEY WORDS

- arrive
- Sir
- clearing
- smell of
- face
- sword

- handle
- leather
- scabbard
- hang (hang-hung-hung)
- magic trick
- wounded

- care for (= take care of)
- curiously
- bundle
- hush
- press
- indoors

Indoors, the house was dark and warm.

The baby stirred in Merlin's arms and whimpered in its sleep.

"A child?" gasped Sir Ector. "What business have I with a baby? I already have one son, and that is enough for me."

"Come close and listen to my story," said Merlin, beckoning with his finger. "This is no ordinary child."

Sir Ector and Kay moved nearer. Merlin shared the secret in whispers until the baby woke and began to cry.

"I will take good care of him," murmured Sir Ector. "It will be an honor to serve my king in this way."

The seasons moved on, and the years passed.
The baby, Arthur, grew into a boy with no idea of who his real parents were.
Arthur's new family kept him hidden away in the forest, and taught him all the things he needed to know.
Sir Ector spent many hours teaching him all the skills he would need in order to become a knight. 

KEY WORDS

- stir
- whimper
- in one's sleep
- gasp
- have business with (have-had-had)
- beckon
- ordinary
- share
- in whispers

- murmur
- serve
- move on
- with no idea of
- hide away (hide-hid-hidden)
- spend (spend-spent-spent)
- in order to
- knight

"Where did I come from?" Arthur asked him as he lifted a heavy sword for the first time. "Who is my real father, and why do I have no mother?"

Sir Ector, whose wife had died giving birth to Kay, pressed a finger to his lips.

"Hush," he said. "Sometimes it is better to know little than to know much."

He jabbed his own sword at Arthur, forcing him to jump aside.

"Well done," said Sir Ector. "A good swordsman must be quick on his feet and never stop watching his enemy."

Kay and Arthur spent many hours learning to fight together. Sometimes Arthur felt as though Kay was actually his enemy, but when the fight was over, they were brothers again.

KEY WORDS

- give birth to (give-gave-given)
- jab
- force
- jump aside
- swordsman
- be quick on one's feet
- enemy
- as though
- edge
- hawk
- perch
- wrist
- halt
- urgently
- hood
- carry
- staff

One day, Arthur and Kay
were out riding their
horses at the edge of
the forest.
Kay wore a heavy
leather glove and a
hawk perched on
his wrist, ready to
hunt rabbits for their
evening meal.
Arthur suddenly
pulled his horse to a
halt.
"Kay!" he called
urgently. "Someone
is watching us. There, in the
shadows, where the forest meets the field. An old man with
a long, grey beard, wearing a hood and carrying a staff."

Kay glanced quickly toward the place where Arthur was pointing.

"I see no one," he declared, and he flung his hawk up into the sky.

"There, I tell you!" Arthur grabbed the reins of Kay's horse and turned it to face the stranger. "You must see him!"
Kay squinted into the sun, searching for his hawk as it became nothing more than a black dot in the sky.

"Arthur, I know who it is, for he has visited us many times since you came to us. Always keeping to the shadows, always hiding among the trees. He is watching over you, seeing that you grow into a good k..."
Kay stopped, unwilling to say more.

KEY WORDS

- glance
- declare
- fling (fling-flung-flung)
- I tell you.
- rein
- stranger

- squint into the sun
- search for
- nothing more than
- dot
- unwilling

"A good what?" asked Arthur.

"A good kind of man," said Kay, but Arthur knew that Kay had intended to say something else.

"Then just tell me his name," begged Arthur, "so that I may greet him next time I see him."

Kay turned to look directly at Arthur.

"Father forbids me to tell you, for there is magic and danger about him."

The mention of *magic* and *danger* sent a chill down Arthur's spine.

"Kay, if you love me as your brother, then please tell me the name of this man."

POP QUIZ

Why did a chill go down Arthur's spine?

ⓐ He was ill and tired.

ⓑ He was excited and nervous.

KEY WORDS

- intend to + *Verb*
- so that
- greet
- directly
- forbid (forbid-forbad-forbidden)
- mention
- send a chill down one's spine
  (send-sent-sent)
- sigh
- swear (swear-swore-sworn)
- grave
- lean forward
- seem
- somewhat
- familiar
- mysterious

Kay sighed. "You swear that you will keep it secret?"

Arthur nodded. "I will take this secret with me to my grave."

Kay leaned forward and pressed his mouth close to Arthur's
ear.

"His name is Merlin."

Arthur didn't think he had heard the name before, but... it
seemed somewhat familiar. But when he turned again to
look at the forest, the mysterious stranger had gone.

Comprehension Quiz

 **A** Match each character with the right explanation.

❶ 

a) lived in the forest with his only son.

❷

b) was the king's wisest advisor.

❸

c) cried when her baby was taken away.

❹ 

d) was the High King of all England.

B Mark T for true or F for false.

❶ Sir Ector and Merlin had met before this occasion. T F

❷ Merlin brought a magic trick to show to Kay. T F

❸ Merlin went indoors to explain the secret. T F

❹ Sir Ector's house was on fire. T F

  Choose the best answer to each question.

❶ Why was Sir Ector the best person to look after Arthur?

a) He lived close to the castle and he was a knight.

b) He lived far from the castle and he was a magician.

c) He lived in London and he was a friend of the king.

d) He lived far from the castle and he knew how to train a knight.

❷ Why were Kay and Sir Ector fighting when Merlin came to them?

a) They were enemies.

b) They had argued about something.

c) The Saxons had invaded their home.

d) Sir Ector was teaching Kay how to fight.

❸ Why do you think Merlin kept coming to watch Arthur?

a) He had been sent as a spy by Arthur's enemies.

b) He had nothing better to do.

c) He wanted to make sure that Arthur was safe.

d) He didn't trust Sir Ector to take care of Arthur.

The True King

As Merlin walked through the forest, his heart was heavy. He had seen that young Arthur was growing strong and healthy, that he was learning new things.

But there was some sad news that Merlin longed to tell the boy, but he could not. King Uther was dead.

Merlin shook his head as he stepped carefully over twisted tree roots. What was the wise thing to do now?

Should he bring Arthur out of hiding and declare him to be the new High King? But who would believe him?

Everyone thought that King Uther had no children, and they would never accept a stranger from the forest.

No, it would have to be something more powerful that brought Arthur to the throne. It would have to be magic.

KEY WORDS

- long to + *Verb*
- step over
- carefully
- twisted
- accept
- powerful

When Merlin reached London, everyone was talking about the death of King Uther.

"With no heir to the throne, anybody could become the High King," they said.

"I'm the strongest," said a man with fiery red hair. "It should be me."

"My mother was the king's sister's husband's friend's cousin," said another man, a shepherd with a couple of lambs. "That makes me a relative of royalty. I should be the new king."

"Then draw your sword and show us what you can do," demanded the first man, and within minutes they were fighting in the marketplace.

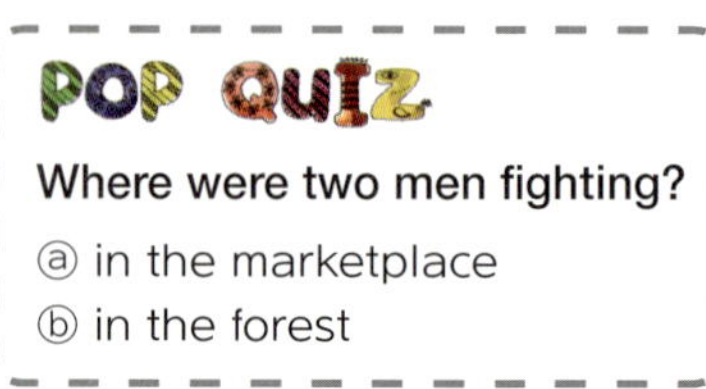

KEY WORDS

- reach
- heir
- strongest
- fiery
- shepherd
- relative
- royalty
- draw (draw-drew-drawn)
- demand
- within minutes
- marketplace
- ring out (ring-rang-rung)
- astonishment
- go round
- catch a glimpse of (catch-caught-caught)

"Stop!" Merlin's voice rang out.

Everybody turned to look at him, their mouths open in astonishment.

"Merlin! It's Merlin!"

The whisper went round the crowd and everyone pressed closer to catch a glimpse of him.

"Who do *you* say should be the new king?" they asked.

"Hand me your sword," Merlin demanded, pointing at the red-haired man.

The man stepped forward and placed his sword in Merlin's outstretched hand.

Merlin waved his hand over the gleaming blade and muttered some words under his breath. The sword grew hot and heavy in his hand, and the crowd gasped as letters of burning gold appeared on the metal.

"Whoever pulls this sword from this stone is the true king of all England," Merlin announced, reading the golden inscription.

"Wait a minute," said the red-haired man. "You said, 'whoever pulls this sword from this *stone*.' What stone?"

"*This* stone!" Merlin declared, striding over to a large rock that stood in the middle of the marketplace and plunging the sword right into the middle of it.

Silence fell.

The shepherd stepped forward and said, "If that sword went into the rock so easily, it must come *out* the same way. Stand aside, everyone, and watch me pull it out."

He grabbed hold of the sword and pulled as hard as he could.  His face turned red and his muscles strained, but the sword didn't move even the tiniest bit.

"I did tell you," Merlin said, "that only the true king of all England will be able to pull it out. Until he comes, the sword will stay exactly where it is."

Weeks passed, and then months. Word spread about the sword, and men came from all over the country to try and remove it from the rock.

But as London grew bigger and busier, people stopped noticing it. Both the rock and the sword were forgotten.

By the time Arthur was fifteen, he was tall and strong.
One day, Sir Ector ordered him to gather provisions and saddle up the horses.

"We're going to London, my lad!" he announced. "Kay is going to fight in his first tournament."

A rush of jealousy made Arthur slow to gather the food and clothing they would need. *He* wanted to fight in a tournament against other young men. *He* wanted to show off his sword skills and prove that he was ready to become a knight.

But he swallowed his jealousy and made sure that everything was ready for the journey.

After all, he'd never been to London before and there might be all kinds of adventures for a young man like him.

Why did Arthur go to London?
ⓐ to try to pull the sword from the stone
ⓑ to help Kay to get ready for a tournament

KEY WORDS

- by the time
- order
- gather
- provisions
- saddle up
- lad

- tournament
- rush
- jealousy
- show off
- prove
- swallow

- make sure
  (make-made-made)
- journey
- after all
- all kinds of
- adventure

It was the smell that hit him first—so many people in one place, with all their filth thrown into the streets. 📖 Aha!

And the *noise*! People shouted to one another, calling out the things they had for sale. Pigs snorted, cows mooed, chickens squawked, and children ran about, shrieking at the tops of their voices. Horses and carts pushed their way along the road, wheels jarring against the stones and leather harnesses creaking.

Arthur looked around in amazement until Kay called, "This way, Arthur!" and pointed towards an open field surrounded by thick crowds.

KEY WORDS

- filth
- **throw** (throw-threw-thrown)
- one another
- call out
- for sale
- snort
- moo
- squawk
- **run about** (run-ran-run)
- shriek
- at the top of one's voice
- cart
- push one's way
- jar
- harness
- creak
- in amazement
- surrounded
- thick
- crowd

Arthur turned his horse's head and rode after Kay.

Kay turned around in his saddle and yelled, "I hope you sharpened my sword well, Arthur!"

Arthur went cold, as though he had fallen through a sheet of ice.

Arthur remembered packing food and ale into the saddlebags, but the sword... Now he remembered. He had seen the sword leaning against the wall, waiting to be sharpened, and he had meant to do it—he really had.

But then Sir Ector had shouted from outside that the pigs had escaped from their pen, and Arthur had run outside to help to catch them.

KEY WORDS

- **ride after** (ride-rode-ridden)
- **saddle**
- **sharpen**
- **go cold**
- **a sheet of ice**
- **pack**

- **ale**
- **saddlebag**
- **mean to +** *Verb* (mean-meant-meant)
- **escape**
- **pen**

And, he realized, as a cold feeling spread right through his body, he had left the sword leaning against the wall.

Kay would be furious! Arthur would have to find a replacement sword—and quickly!

"Kay!" he called. "I'll meet you at the tournament field in a few minutes. There's something I need to do."

He leapt off his horse and handed the reins to a blushing girl.

"Hold my horse for me, will you?" he said, looking wildly around. "I won't be long."

Where could he possibly find a sword? There must be someone who could lend him one, or even sell him one.

▲ ale

POP QUIZ

What did Arthur forget to take to London?
ⓐ a sword
ⓑ a pig

KEY WORDS

- furious
- replacement
- leap off (leap-leapt-leapt)
- blushing
- wildly
- I won't be long.
- possibly
- lend (lend-lent-lent)

A large woman with a basket full of bread knocked him over, and Arthur fell against a rock. Pain shot through him first, but astonishment quickly followed.

Sticking out of the rock was a sword! Who did it belong to, and why was it here?

But there was no time to find out—he needed it now, and he would put it back later.

Arthur reached out and pulled the sword out of the rock. It slid out smoothly, like a warm knife through butter.

As Arthur held it up, smiling, the sun glinted off some writing along the blade. But he didn't have a chance to read it because someone screamed, right by his ear.

It was the woman with the basket—which was now in the mud, loaves of bread spilling out of it—pressing her hands to her cheeks.

"He pulled the sword out of the rock!" she screeched. "He's the true king of all England!"

Some people ignored her and kept walking, but a few stopped and stared.

KEY WORDS

- knock over
- fall against
- **shoot** (shoot-shot-shot)
- stick out of
- belong to
- **slide out** (slide-slid-slid)
- smoothly
- glint
- chance
- loaves
- spill out of
- screech
- ignore
- stare

First one, then another dropped to their knees and bowed their heads. 

Words rippled through the crowd, first a whisper and then a shout.

"It's the King! We have a new High King at last!"

Arthur looked round, bewildered, as every face looked towards him—some hopeful, some angry, others simply confused, as he was.

But then a man pushed through the crowd, a huge smile above his long grey beard.

"I'm Merlin and I'm here to serve you," he announced.

"Welcome to London, Arthur. We have work to do."

KEY WORDS

- drop to one's knees
- bow
- ripple
- at last

- bewildered
- confused
- push through the crowd

Comprehension Quiz

A Match each line with the right character.

 ❶ 

Merlin

• a) "I'm related to the king."

❷ 

Sir Ector

• b) "Hand me your sword. "

❸ 

shepherd

• c) "Let's go to London."

B Mark T for true or F for false.

❶ Merlin stabbed a man with his sword.　　　T　F

❷ For the shepherd, the sword came out of the rock
as easily as it went in.　　　T　F

❸ The sword and the rock were hidden in the forest.　　　T　F

❹ Arthur was fifteen years old when he pulled the sword
out of the rock.　　　T　F

❶ Why did some men try to pull the sword out of the stone?

a) Each one wanted a new sword.

b) Each one wanted to show that he was strong.

c) Each one wanted to be the new king of England.

d) Each one wanted to prove that the sword was not magical.

❷ Why hadn't Arthur brought Kay's sword?

a) He had been distracted while he was packing everything.

b) He wanted Kay to lose the tournament.

c) He had sent it away to be sharpened.

d) He had used it to help to catch the pigs.

D Circle the right word for each underlined part.

❶ Arthur was the (first / second / third) person to pull the sword out of the rock.

❷ The woman with the basket pressed her (loaves / hands / mud) to her cheeks.

❸ People in the crowd dropped to their (hands / feet / knees) and bowed their heads.

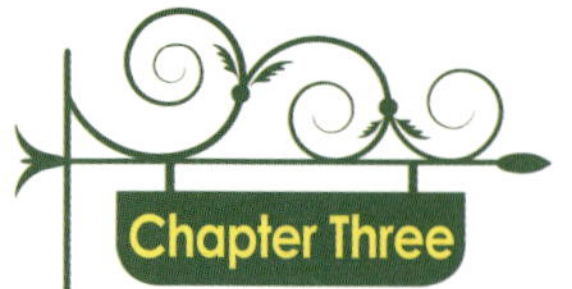

The Kingdom of Camelot

Not everyone was pleased that a new High King had been found. Aha!

There were already eleven other kings in England, each with a small kingdom, and they were not happy about the new king, because they wanted to be free to rule their own kingdoms. They plotted against King Arthur and began to raise armies to fight against him.

"What shall I do?" Arthur asked Merlin. "I cannot defeat all eleven kings at once."

"I know of something that will help you," promised Merlin. "Meet me tonight, outside the castle walls."

The moon was full when Arthur crept out that night.

"Where are we going?" he whispered.

Merlin pressed a finger to his lips and gave a low whistle. Two white horses cantered out of the darkness and Merlin swung himself into the saddle of the first one.

"We must make haste," he said, "and make sure that we are not followed."

He spurred his horse into a trot and disappeared into the darkness.

KEY WORDS

- rule
- plot against
- raise army
- defeat
- at once
- full
- creep out (creep-crept-crept)

- give a whistle
- canter
- darkness
- swing (swing-swung-swung)
- make haste
- spur
- trot

"Wait for me!" hissed Arthur as he climbed onto the second horse and set off after the glimmer of white that was Merlin's horse.

He and Merlin rode through the darkness for what seemed like hours, yet when Merlin pulled up his horse by the side of a lake, the moon was still high, spilling its wintry light across the water.

"What is this place?" murmured Arthur.

"Out there"—Merlin pointed with a finger—"is the enchanted island of Avalon. Three queens live there, as they have done since ancient times."

Arthur swallowed. More magic. Perhaps he should have stayed in London.

KEY WORDS

- hiss
- set off (set-set-set)
- glimmer
- pull up
- still
- spill
- wintry
- enchanted
- ancient times
- swallow
- perhaps

A small, wooden boat
was pulled up on the
shore of the lake,
with a pair of oars
lying in it.
Merlin and Arthur
dismounted their
horses and stepped
into the boat.
A faint mist lay on
the surface of the
water, swirling around

them as Arthur rowed out into the middle of the lake.
Merlin held up a hand, palm outwards. "Stop here."
Arthur did as he was told, dipping the oars into the water
now and again to make sure the boat didn't drift away.

KEY WORDS

- shore
- oar
- lying
- **dismount** (↔ mount)
- faint
- mist
- **lie** (lie‑lay‑lain)

- surface
- swirl
- row
- dip
- now and again
- drift away

Everything was completely still; not a breath of wind disturbed the dark water.

Suddenly, something launched itself out of the water—a milky-white hand, its fingers clasped around a sword in a golden scabbard.

"The Lady of the Lake," said Merlin in a low voice. "Take the sword from her hand."

Arthur leaned forward, trembling, and took the sword.

There was a sound like a gentle sigh and all the grasses along the lake shore shivered.

The hand disappeared into the water, and Arthur was left wondering if he had dreamed the whole thing. But there was the sword and scabbard in his hand. He looked up at Merlin questioningly.

"The name of the sword is Excalibur," said Merlin. "It has magical qualities, of course, and so does the scabbard."

"M… magical qualities?" said Arthur.

"Indeed." Merlin nodded solemnly. "If you use Excalibur in a battle, you will always defeat your opponent."

KEY WORDS

- completely
- a breath of wind
- disturb
- launch
- milky-white
- clasp
- tremble
- shiver

- wonder
- if
- questioningly
- quality
- indeed
- solemnly
- battle
- opponent

"What about the scabbard?"

"As long as you wear the scabbard, you will be protected from any harm to your own body."

Arthur looked down at the scabbard in his hand.

"Invincible," he murmured to himself. "Nobody will be able to defeat me."

And the words that Arthur had murmured to himself by the lake came true.

One by one, each of the eleven kings brought an army to fight against Arthur. The battles were fierce, and blood was spilled, but none of it was Arthur's.

At last, all the eleven kings were forced to admit defeat. Each one bowed to Arthur on one knee and offered him their service as the High King of all England. Arthur accepted them all as his subjects.

KEY WORDS

- as long as
- harm
- invincible
- come true
  (come-came-come)
- one by one
- fierce
- none
- admit
- offer
- accept
- subject
- set up
- base
- justice
- retreat
- be done
- for now
- marry
- bride

And so peace came to England.

Arthur set up his base in the castle of Camelot. It became known as a place of joy and celebration, of justice and peace. Merlin retreated to a quiet place, knowing that his work was done, for now.

Arthur grew into a fine man, who ruled his kingdom well. He married a beautiful French bride called Guinevere.

Every knight in the country wanted to serve King Arthur and live at the court of Camelot, but Arthur chose only the best and most loyal.

Their names were on the lips of every man, woman and child, spoken with awe and wonder. Sir Lancelot, Sir Gawain, Sir Galahad, Sir Bedevere...

Queen Guinevere's father wanted to give a wedding present to the newly married couple.

"Let me give you a huge table, made of the finest and most solid wood," he said. "You will need a place for all your knights to sit with you and to discuss battle plans together."

Arthur agreed.

"But let it be a round table," he said. "If all my knights sit with me at a round table, none will feel more favoured than another. All will be equal."

And so the immense table was brought to Camelot.

When the knights sat round it, none of them could say, "I am more important than you because I sit at the end of the table, opposite the king."

The Knights of the Round Table carried out many brave acts in the name of the king.

They fought against the Saxons when they tried to invade England yet again, forcing them back to their own land. They fought against new invaders—the Romans.

The Romans had conquered most of Europe and wanted England as well.

The knights held regular tournaments in order to practice their skills. They fought one another with swords and other weapons; they took part in jousting contests, charging at each other on horseback and trying to knock each other off with long lances.

They rescued young women who were held captive or had other problems that they needed help with.

POP QUIZ

Mark T for true or F for false.

The women rescued the knights who were in trouble. T / F

KEY WORDS

- invade
- yet again
- Roman
- conquer
- weapon
- take part in (take-took-taken)
- joust
- charge at
- knock off
- lance

- rescue
- be held captive
- beast
- closest
- glory
- praise
- rejoice
- in safe hands
- that is
- except

Some say that they even battled against dragons and other magical beasts that lived in England in those days.

Sir Lancelot became Arthur's closest friend, and they spent many hours together, talking about battles and rescues, and the glories of Camelot.

King Arthur and his knights were praised across the land, as all the people rejoiced that the kingdom was in safe hands.

All the people, that is, except one man named Mordred.

A Match each character with the right explanation.

Guinevere

Sir Lancelot

Merlin

a) I left Arthur alone to rule his kingdom in peace.

b) I am a brave knight, and I am the king's best friend.

c) My father gave the Round Table to my husband and me as a gift.

B Mark T for true or F for false.

1. The boat was made out of wood. T F

2. The boat had a small leak. T F

3. The boat was broken in the middle of the lake. T F

4. The boat had two oars in it. T F

C

C Choose the best answer to each question.

❶ Why were the other kings unhappy when Arthur was declared the king of all England?

a) They thought that he was too young to be a king.

b) They did not want anyone to rule over them.

c) They thought that he was not really the son of King Uther.

d) They did not think that there should be any kings in England.

❷ Why was the table round?

a) so that it could be rolled along the ground

b) so that it would fit into the room more easily

c) so that more people could sit round it

d) so that no knight would feel more important than any of the others

D Put the sentences in order.

❶ Merlin gave a low whistle.

❷ Merlin and his horse trotted away.

❸ Arthur and Merlin met outside the castle wall.

❹ Two white horses came out of the darkness.

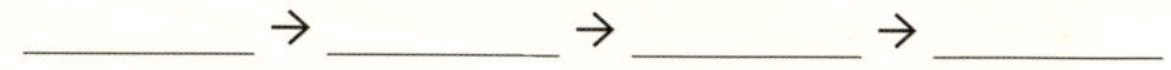

_________ → _________ → _________ → _________

Chapter Four

Betrayal

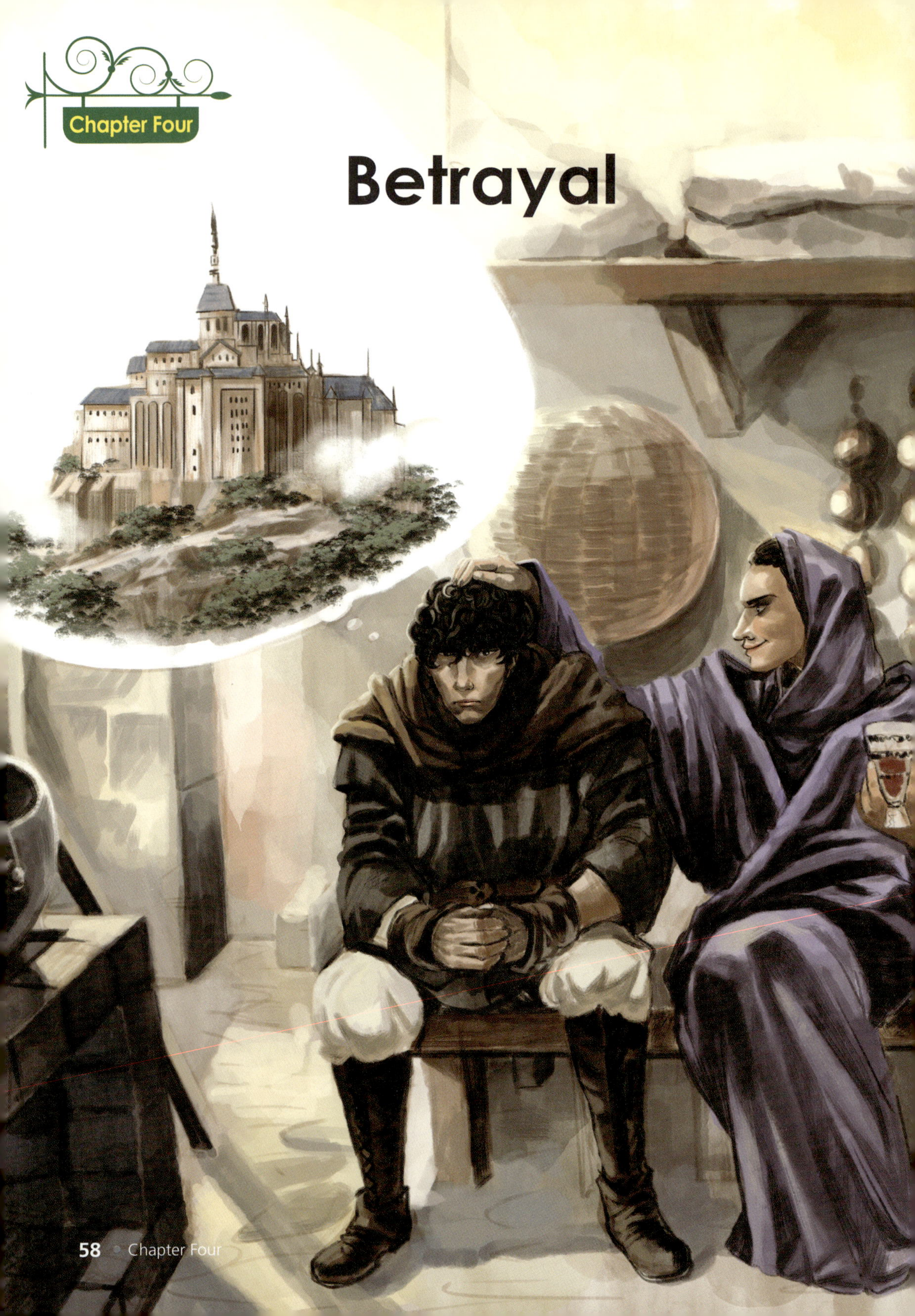

Mordred was intensely jealous of Arthur.

"*I* should be the High King," he muttered to himself. "I have all the skills of a knight, and the throne is truly mine."

"Indeed it is," said his mother, Morgana, stroking his thick, black hair.

"As I have told you many times, Queen Igraine was *my* mother too. The old King Uther killed my father in order to marry Igraine, and I was sent away. They say that she then had a baby, Arthur, but who knows whether that is the truth? This King Arthur may be an imposter! Mordred, my love, *you* should be the king."

"I will go to Camelot," he said, "and I will become one of the Knights of the Round Table. I will gain the confidence of the king and of Guinevere, his queen."

Morgana nodded and smiled.

What was the name of Mordred's mother?
ⓐ Igraine
ⓑ Morgana

KEY WORDS

- intensely
- jealous
- stroke
- whether
- imposter
- gain
- confidence

A few days later, one of Arthur's servants entered the throne room at Camelot.

"A new knight had arrived to seek the favour of the king," he announced.

"Let him compete at the tournaments with all the other knights," said Arthur. "That way, I can judge fairly between them all."

"But this knight says that he is your nephew," the servant went on.

"My *nephew*?" said Arthur, puzzled. "But I have no brothers or sisters that I know of."

His heart began to beat faster—was it possible that he *did* have some family, after all? If it was true, how he longed to know them!

KEY WORDS

- servant
- throne room
- seek
- favour
- compete
- judge
- fairly

- nephew
- puzzled
- **show someone in** (show-showed-shown)
- coal-black
- curl
- about by the wind
- your majesty

A young man was shown in, his coal-black curls blown about by the wind. He removed his sword from his scabbard and offered it to Arthur, bowing low at the same time.

"Your majesty," he said, "I am Mordred, the son of your sister, Morgana, daughter of Igraine. I offer you my service and my sword, so that I may fight for you and serve you in this kingdom of Camelot."

"Mordred, you may rise," said Arthur. "I shall be honoured
to have you in my service."

He didn't see the sly grin that crept over Mordred's face, or
the glitter in his eye.

"Thank you, your majesty," said Mordred. "I swear that I
will stay close by you until the day you die."

Queen Guinevere liked to watch the knights training together,
and competing at tournaments.
There was one knight in particular who caught her eye.
His name was Sir Lancelot. He was French, just as she was,
and his voice reminded her of home.

Whenever there was a tournament, he bowed to her before he started to compete in the arena, and she smiled back. Arthur was very busy making sure that England was well defended, and he did not notice that his wife and his best friend, Sir Lancelot, were gradually falling in love.

But Mordred noticed. He nodded and smiled to himself, storing up the information until it might be useful.

That summer, Sir Lancelot and Queen Guinevere spent more and more time together.

One day, the queen stumbled and almost fell, but Sir
Lancelot reached out and grabbed her hand to steady her.
Guinevere flushed pink and stammered her thanks, but she
did not let go of Sir Lancelot's hand.
Lancelot gazed into her eyes.

"My queen," he murmured, "I cannot conceal my feelings for you any longer."
"Hush," whispered Guinevere and she leaned in to kiss him.
Mordred, hidden behind a nearby tree, watched it all.

A few days later, Arthur was in his throne room, consulting with his advisors.

"Where is my wife?" he demanded. "I have not seen her all morning and I wish to speak with her."

The advisors looked at one another and shrugged their shoulders.

"We have not seen her. Perhaps she is instructing the cooks about the evening meal."

"No, she is not." Mordred stepped forward.

"Then where is she?" Arthur snapped, his anxiety making him angry.

"Perhaps it is better that I tell you in private," said Mordred.

Arthur nodded, and waved his advisors away.

KEY WORDS

- stumble
- steady
- flush
- stammer
- let go of
- gaze into
- conceal
- any longer
- consult with
- advisor
- shrug one's shoulder
- instruct
- cook
- snap
- anxiety
- in private
- wave away

"Now then, tell me where she is!" he demanded.

In reply, Mordred drew Arthur to the window, which looked down over the river bank.

He pointed at a pair of figures half shadowed by the trees.

"Where?" asked Arthur. "I see nothing down there but a pair of young lovers..."

His voice faded as he looked more closely.

There was no doubt about it—the woman who ran out of the shadows into the sunlight, laughing as a man caught hold of her and kissed her, was Guinevere. And the man was his best friend, Sir Lancelot.

With a roar that made the dogs in the kennels bark in fear, Arthur grabbed his sword. He raced down the spiral staircase, across the courtyard and into the stables.

KEY WORDS

- in reply
- figure
- lover
- fade
- no doubt
- catch hold of
- roar
- kennel

- bark
- spiral
- staircase
- courtyard
- stable
- leap onto (↔ leap off)
- gallop
- scatter

"Saddle my horse!" he demanded.

The moment the horse was ready, he leapt onto its back and galloped out of the castle gates, scattering people and animals as he went.

His knights, just returned from training on the tournament field, turned their horses after him and followed their king.

Arthur grasped Excalibur tightly, ready to fight.

There, ahead of him, was that traitor, Sir Lancelot, scooping Guinevere onto his horse and galloping away along the river bank. He would not escape.

Raising Excalibur high above his head, Arthur gave the command to his knights and they urged their horses to gallop faster.

"Bring them to me!" he shouted. "They shall both be sentenced to death!"

A couple of hours later, Arthur was in his throne room with Mordred.

"How could they betray me like this?" he said.

"Your majesty, there are always traitors in the king's court," said Mordred.

Arthur rested a hand on his nephew's shoulder.

"Then I am glad to have you with me," he said. "I would trust you with my life."

There was a clattering of hooves in the courtyard below, and the sound of voices shouting.

Mordred went to the window.

"Let me go and find out what is happening. Wait here, your majesty."

KEY WORDS

- grasp
- ahead of
- traitor
- scoop
- give a command
- urge
- be sentenced to death
- betray
- rest
- clattering
- hooves

A few minutes later, Mordred returned.

"They have brought the queen, but Sir Lancelot is not with them."

"Where is he?" shouted Arthur. "I will kill him myself if I find him."

"Nobody knows, your majesty, but the queen will be placed in the dungeon."

Arthur pressed his hand to his face to hide his tears.

"Where is Merlin when I need his help?" he wondered.

He couldn't bear the thought of his beautiful Guinevere rotting in a dark, underground prison.

KEY WORDS

- dungeon
- **bear** (bear-bore-borne)
- rot
- underground
- prison
- rather
- bedchamber

- toss and turn
- drift
- discover
- stage
- rescue
- homeland

"No. Rather let her be kept to her bedchamber and be guarded day and night," he said.

Arthur didn't sleep well that night. He tossed and turned on his bed, drifting in and out of dreams.

It wasn't until the morning that Arthur discovered that Guinevere was gone.

Sir Lancelot had staged a rescue in the middle of the night, and had taken her away to France, back to their homeland.

Arthur leapt from his bed and called for food, armour and a good horse.

"I will follow them myself," he announced, "and I will take my loyal knights with me. This time, neither of them shall escape the sword."

"But who will watch over the kingdom while you are gone?" asked Mordred, his face twisting in concern.

"You shall, my dear nephew," said Arthur. "Perhaps you are the only one I can truly trust."

Mordred bowed as low as he could, to hide the secret smile on his face. 

"I shall rule the kingdom as though it is my own," he promised.

KEY WORDS

- call for
- armour
- neither
- twist
- in concern

A Mark T for true or F for false.

1. Igraine was Morgana's mother. T F
2. Igraine was Arthur's mother. T F
3. Uther was Morgana's father. T F
4. Mordred was Morgana's son. T F

B Match each place with the right event.

1. By the river,   •　　• a) Arthur talked to his advisors.

2. Behind a tree,   •　　• b) Sir Lancelot and Guinevere shared a kiss.

3. In the throne room, •　　• c) Mordred spied on Sir Lancelot and Guinevere.

4. At the window,   •　　• d) Arthur saw Sir Lancelot and Guinevere together.

 Choose the best answer to each question.

1 How did King Arthur choose the best knights to serve him at Camelot?

a) He chose the most handsome men.

b) He chose the knights that performed best in the tournaments.

c) He asked his wife, Guinevere, to choose the knights.

d) He only chose the knights that were his relatives.

2 Why didn't Arthur notice that Guinevere and Sir Lancelot were falling in love?

a) He never spent any time with them.

b) He was away in France.

c) His eyesight was poor.

d) He was very busy to look after his kingdom.

3 Why did Mordred hide a "secret smile"?

a) Because he was free to go home to his mother.

b) Because he loved Arthur with all his heart.

c) Because he had succeeded in making Arthur trust him.

d) Because he was going to France with Arthur.

Chapter Five

The Final Battle

It was a long journey to France, and Arthur was away for many weeks.

Mordred ruled the kingdom well, and people liked him.

“After all,” he told them, “I am the heir to the throne. Arthur has no sons, and I am his nearest living relative. One day I shall be your king.”

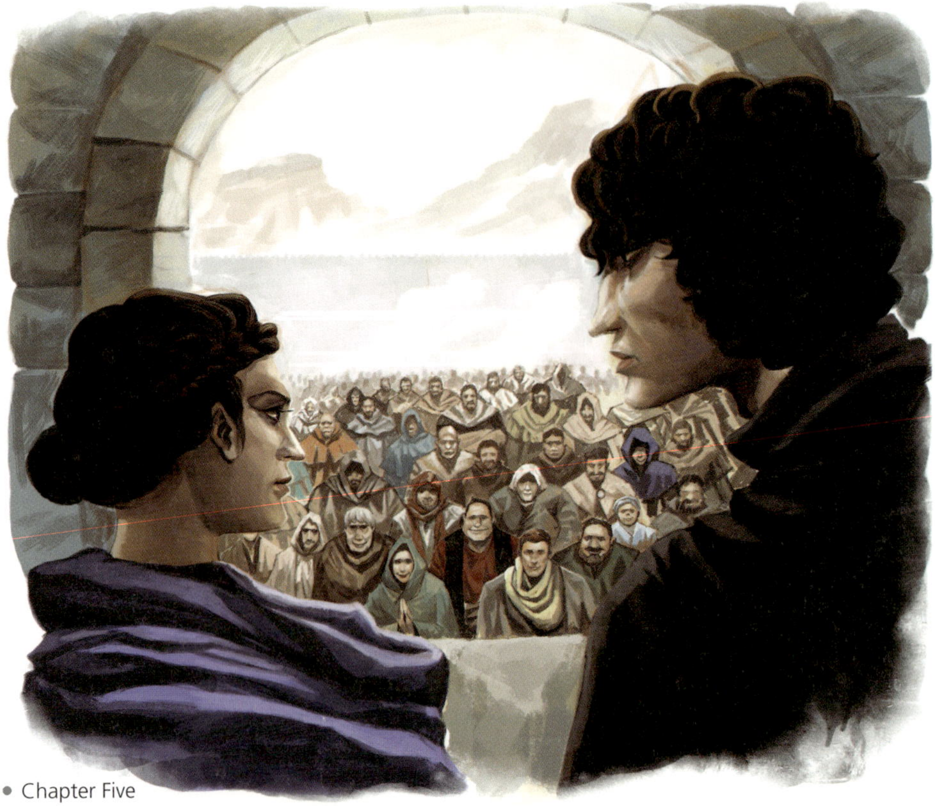

The weeks passed, and turned into months. There was no news from Arthur, so Mordred decided that it was time to put the next stage of his plan into action.

"Arthur is dead," he announced, making sure that he kept a sad expression on his face.

The people believed him, and although they mourned King Arthur, they rejoiced that a good king was already waiting to take his place.

Mordred gave the people money and raised an army that was loyal to him.

Everyone loved him, and he acted as though Camelot and the whole of England belonged to him.

Mordred's mother, Morgana, ruled alongside him.

Why did Mordred tell the people that Arthur was dead?

ⓐ He believed it was the truth.
ⓑ He wanted to be the king of England.

KEY WORDS

- nearest
- put ~ into action
- expression

- mourn
- take one's place
- alongside

King Arthur returned from France in a fury with his loyal knights. But when he tried to return to Camelot to regain his throne, he found the way blocked by soldiers.

"How dare you raise your weapons to me, your true king!" he said.

Mordred and Morgana came out to meet him.

"You are defeated," declared Mordred, as his army cheered. "The people have chosen *me* to be their king."

"Then the people are wrong," muttered Arthur. "It is God who chooses a king, not the people."

Arthur and his knights rode up and down the country, gathering the people who remained loyal to him. They managed to raise a new army, and Arthur declared war on Mordred.

KEY WORDS

- in a fury
- regain
- how dare
- cheer
- remain
- manage
- battlefield
- row upon row of
- in case
- reason with
- soothing
- thigh

The two armies met on the battlefield, row upon row of men
and horses facing one another.

Arthur rode forward to meet Mordred and Morgana,
Excalibur raised in case he needed to defend himself.

Morgana tried to reason with him.

"Arthur, my dear brother," she said in a soothing voice. "We
should not be fighting. We are part of the same family, after
all."

She reached forward and rested a hand on Arthur's thigh.

"Families should not betray one another," snapped Arthur, pulling away. "Justice will be done today."

And he galloped away, back to his army.

"What a shame," said Morgana smoothly as she held up the jewelled scabbard that Arthur carried everywhere. "He seems to have forgotten something."

Then she burst into wicked laughter. "He is invincible no more! To battle!"

With shouts of rage and courage, the two armies approached each other, and the battle began. It was a day filled with blood and death, as soldiers on both sides fell to the ground.

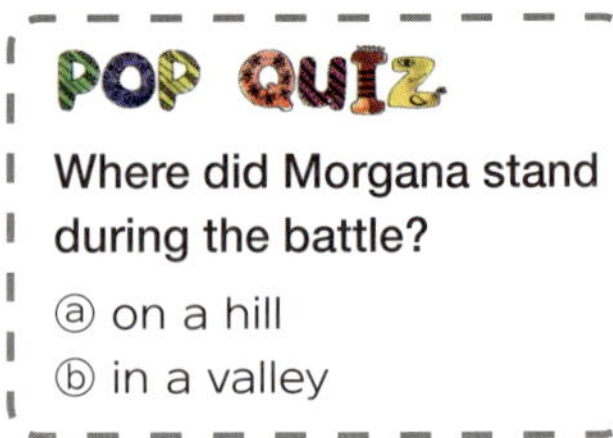

KEY WORDS

- pull away
- What a shame!
- jewelled
- burst into laughter
- wicked
- rage

- courage
- approach
- sink
- bloodstained
- nothing but
- shield

- apart
- hilltop
- dazzle
- setting sun

The hours passed and the sun began to sink lower, so that the sky became as red as the bloodstained fields.

By the end of the day, only a few men had survived, and Arthur and Mordred were among them.

They faced one another at last, with nothing but their swords and shields to defend them.

Morgana stood apart, on a hilltop, raising something in her hand—something that was dazzling as it caught the light of the setting sun.

"My scabbard!" gasped Arthur, just as Mordred raised his sword and brought it down with a mighty swing.

Just in time, Arthur lifted his shield above his head and the force of the blow sent a sharp pain through his shoulder. There was no time to realize that he could, after all, be killed in this fight.

Arthur focused all his energy on the battle and trusted Excalibur to work its magic.

But Arthur was growing tired, and he could hardly get his breath. His armour seemed to weigh him down, pulling him towards the earth, but he charged into Mordred, knocking him over so that Mordred's helmet tumbled off. **Aha!**

KEY WORDS

- mighty
- just in time
- blow
- sharp
- hardly

- get one's breath (get-got-gotten)
- weigh ~ down
- earth
- charge into
- tumble off

Mordred staggered to his feet.

"I *will* be the king," he gasped, his face smeared with dirt and blood so that he looked like a mad man. He stabbed his sword into the gap at the neck of Arthur's breastplate, and drove it in deep.

Arthur cried out in pain and dismay, but managed to bring Excalibur down hard on Mordred's unprotected head. There was a sickening crack, and a surprised look crossed Mordred's face. He sank down, almost pulling Arthur with him into the dirt. Mordred didn't move again.

KEY WORDS

- stagger to one's feet
- smear with
- mad
- stab
- gap
- neck
- breastplate
- **drive** (drive-drove-driven)

- cry out
- in dismay
- **bring down** (bring-brought-brought)
- unprotected
- sickening
- crack
- cross
- **sink down** (sink-sank-sunk)

There was a scream from the hill and Arthur glanced up to see Morgana fall to her knees.

He couldn't stand up any longer and toppled into the dirt, still clutching Excalibur.

"Your majesty, my king! You cannot die!"

It was Sir Bedevere, running to Arthur's aid and crouching at his side.

Arthur shook his head, gasping at the pain.

"You are wrong, my friend. Death comes to us all in the end."

"My lord, what shall I do?"

Sir Bedevere cradled Arthur's head in his hands, tears streaming down his cheeks.

KEY WORDS

- fall to one's knees
- topple
- clutch
- run to one's aid
- crouch
- in the end
- lord
- tears stream down one's cheeks[face]

"You must take me to the lake," croaked Arthur. "The lake where Excalibur was given to me."

"What lake?" asked Sir Bedevere. "Where is it? Tell me and I will gladly take you there as my last act of service."

"I do not have much time left to me."

Arthur's voice was growing fainter.

"Leave me here and take Excalibur. It must be returned to the Lady of the Lake."

"No, no," protested Sir Bedevere, "I will take both you and your sword, but my king, you must tell me how to find it!"

"*I* know the way," said a voice.

Sir Bedevere looked up to see an old man with a beard and a wooden staff.

"Merlin!" he gasped. "We have not seen you for many years. Where have you been?"

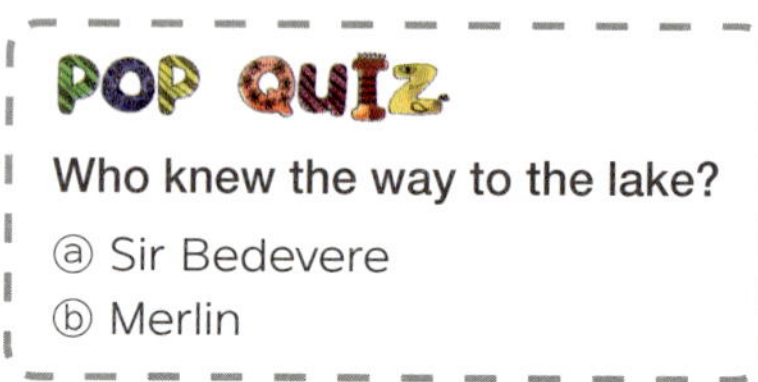

KEY WORDS

- croak
- gladly
- fainter
- protest
- for many years
- in front of
- calm
- as ever
- beneath

"Arthur needed to learn how to rule for himself," explained Merlin. "He could not have done that if I had been at his shoulder all the time. But I watched over him, as I have watched all his life."

Between them, Sir Bedevere and Merlin managed to lift Arthur so that he lay across his horse.

Slowly, carefully, they led the horse to the lake.

As they came out of the forest, there in front of them was the lake, calm as ever beneath the evening sky.

The boat was pulled up on the shore, just as before, and the mist crept over the surface of the lake.

"Help me to get him into the boat," said Merlin.

Sir Bedevere supported Arthur as he slid off the horse's back. Once he was in the boat, Merlin got in too, and pushed it away from the shore.

"Where are you taking him?" asked Sir Bedevere.

Merlin waved towards the center of the lake, where the mist was thickest.

"To the island of Avalon," he said, "where he may rest in peace."

The boat slipped away, silent on the still water, making barely a ripple.

After a while it stopped, as though invisible hands held it, and there appeared the milky-white hand of the Lady of the Lake.

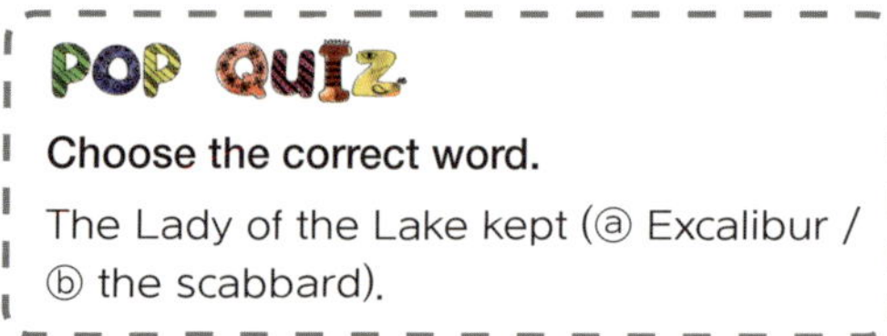

KEY WORDS

- support
- once
- thickest
- slip away
- barely
- invisible
- salute
- fallen

Merlin handed Excalibur to her and she held it high for a moment, saluting the fallen king.

Then she was gone, and the boat sailed on into the mist toward the island of Avalon.

And there Arthur rests to this day, though none have found his grave.

But some do say that he lives there still, waiting for the right moment to return and take his throne, when England needs him most.

A Match each character with the right action.

Morgana

Mordred

- a) stabbed Arthur in the neck.

- b) stole Arthur's scabbard.

- c) burst into wicked laughter.

- d) lost his/her helmet on the battlefield.

B Mark T for true or F for false.

❶ Merlin handed Excalibur to the Lady of the Lake.   T F

❷ The boat was blown across the water by a strong wind.   T F

❸ Nobody ever found Arthur's grave.   T F

C Circle the right word for each underlined part.

❶ Arthur wanted his (wife / throne / horse) back, but Mordred's (mother / knights / soldiers) blocked the way.

❷ The two (armies / friends / castles) met on the battlefield, mounted on (spears / horses / swords).

 Choose the best answer to each question.

❶ What did Arthur do first when Mordred prevented him from returning to his throne?

a) He went back to France.

b) He raised an army of people from all over the country.

c) He attacked Camelot with the help of his knights.

d) He set fire to Camelot.

❷ Why did Morgana fall to her knees?

a) She was saying a prayer.

b) She was wounded by a sword.

c) She was too tired to stand up any longer.

d) She was upset by Mordred's death.

E Put the sentences in order.

❶ Arthur lifted his shield to protect himself.

❷ Morgana was on a hilltop, holding up the scabbard.

❸ Mordred brought down his sword toward Arthur's head.

❹ Arthur realized that Morgana had his scabbard.

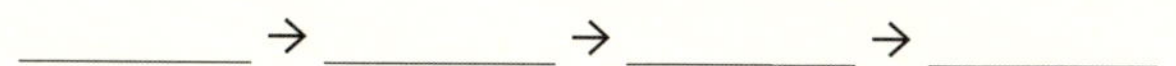

_________ → _________ → _________ → _________

Let's Review the Story

Fill in the blanks to review the story.

Title: King ______

Chapter 1: The heir to the throne of all England is a baby called ______. ______ hides him away with Sir ______ and his son, ______. Arthur grows up with them in secret.

Chapter 2: The ______ of all England dies. Merlin puts an enchanted sword into a ______ and declares that only the true king of all ______ will be able to ______ it out. When Arthur is ______ years old, he pulls it out and becomes the king.

Chapter 3: To make sure that Arthur wins his battles, ______ takes him to a mysterious ______, where he is given a sword called ______ and a magical ______ by the Lady of the Lake. Arthur marries ______ and gathers loyal ______ around him, including his best friend, Sir ______.

Chapter 4: Arthur's nephew, ______, wants to be the king of all England. When Sir Lancelot and Guinevere fall in ______ and run away to ______, Arthur follows them. He leaves ______ in charge of the kingdom.

Chapter 5: When Arthur returns from ______, Mordred has made himself the king of all England. Arthur must battle Mordred and his army. Before the battle, Morgana steals Arthur's ______. Arthur kills ______, but is also wounded himself. Merlin takes the dying Arthur to the island of ______, where he may have died ... or he may still be alive!

Let's Think & Talk

Think about the following questions and answer them freely.

❶ King Arthur could win all the battles thanks to his magical sword, Excalibur. If some magical power was also given to you, what would you use it for and why?

❷ Why did King Arthur make the knights' table round? In what circumstances do we need such an idea in our lives?

❸ Sir Lancelot finally chose love over friendship. If you had been in his shoes, what choice would you have made?

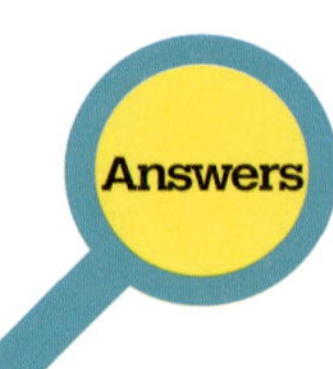

Let's Review the Story

Title: King Arthur

Chapter 1: The heir to the throne of all England is a baby called Arthur . Merlin hides him away with Sir Ector and his son, Kay . Arthur grows up with them in secret.

Chapter 2: The king of all England dies. Merlin puts an enchanted sword into a rock and declares that only the true king of all England will be able to pull it out. When Arthur is fifteen years old, he pulls it out and becomes the king.

Chapter 3: To make sure that Arthur wins his battles, Merlin takes him to a mysterious lake , where he is given a sword called Excalibur and a magical scabbard by the Lady of the Lake. Arthur marries Guinevere and gathers loyal knights around him, including his best friend, Sir Lancelot .

Chapter 4: Arthur's nephew, Mordred , wants to be the king of all England. When Sir Lancelot and Guinevere fall in love and run away to France , Arthur follows them. He leaves Mordred in charge of the kingdom.

Chapter 5: When Arthur returns from France , Mordred has made himself the king of all England. Arthur must battle Mordred and his army. Before the battle, Morgana steals Arthur's scabbard . Arthur kills Mordred , but is also wounded himself. Merlin takes the dying Arthur to the island of Avalon , where he may have died ... or he may still be alive!

After-reading Test

- King Arthur
- Level 5
- 30 Questions

(Vocabulary 7 / Reading Comprehension 16 /

Sentence Structure & Grammar 7)

1. What is a "scabbard"?
   ① a wound
   ② a sword holder
   ③ a weapon
   ④ a secret

2. Which of the following is the wrong past tense form of the verb?
   ① knelt
   ② flung
   ③ swore
   ④ lend

3. What does the word "invincible" mean?
   ① Nobody could see him.
   ② Nobody could hear him.
   ③ Nobody could defeat him.
   ④ Nobody could remember him.

4. Which of the following is the wrong plural form?
   ① loaves
   ② hoofes
   ③ knights
   ④ servants

5. Which of the following is similar to the words "care for"?

   Or a wounded animal to care for?

   ① take care of
   ② move on
   ③ jump aside
   ④ search for

6. What is the common word for the two blanks?

> • His face smeared ____________ dirt.
> • Morgana tried to reason ____________ him.

① on   ② to
③ for   ④ with

7. What are the proper words for the blanks?

> • He charged ____________ Mordred.
> • They took part ____________ jousting contests.
> • They shall both be sentenced ____________ death!

① in – for – on   ② of – to – with
③ into – in – to   ④ with – in – for

8. Why was England a "wild and dangerous place"? Choose two answers.
   ① There were many wild animals.
   ② The kings of different areas fought each other.
   ③ The Saxons came to invade England.
   ④ The weather was very unpleasant.

9. Why did Kay say that he could NOT see Merlin standing in the shadows?
   ① His eyesight was poor.
   ② The forest was too dark.
   ③ He was pretending not to see him.
   ④ The sun was in his eyes.

10. What magically appeared on the red-haired man's sword?
    ① a crown   ② two lambs
    ③ a stone   ④ some writing

11. Why was Arthur jealous of Kay?
① Kay was more handsome than Arthur.
② Arthur wanted to fight in the tournament.
③ Kay had more food than Arthur.
④ More girls liked Kay than liked Arthur.

12. Why did the woman with the basket scream when Arthur pulled the sword
out of the rock?
① She thought that Arthur was going to kill her.
② She was angry because Arthur had spilled her bread.
③ She realized that Arthur must be the true king of all England.
④ She wanted everyone to know that Arthur was stealing the sword.

13. Why did Merlin leave Camelot?
① Arthur told him to go away.
② He was scared of the eleven kings.
③ His work was done, for a while.
④ He did not want to serve Arthur.

14. Why did the knights hold tournaments?
① They wanted to hurt each other.
② They wanted to improve their skills.
③ They wanted to impress young women.
④ They wanted to invite the Saxons to join in.

15. According to the people, of these things which did the knights NOT do?
① They rescued women.
② They fought against dragons.
③ They raced against horses.
④ They held jousting contests.

16. **Why did Mordred think that he should be the king? Choose two answers.**
① He had all the correct skills to be a king.
② His mother was King Arthur's sister.
③ He was born in Camelot.
④ He was braver than all the other knights.

17. **Why did Arthur's heart "beat faster" when he heard that Mordred was his nephew?**
① He was excited at the thought that he might have some living relatives.
② He was afraid that Mordred had come to fight against him.
③ He was getting old and he was not healthy.
④ He was angry that Mordred wanted to be a knight without taking part in a tournament.

18. **Why did Mordred have a "sly grin on his face" and a "glitter in his eye"?**
① He was happy to serve Arthur.
② He had a secret plan to become the king.
③ He wanted to marry Guinevere.
④ He was crying at the thought of leaving his mother.

19. **Why did the people of England like Mordred? Choose two answers.**
① He invited them to parties at the castle.
② They thought that he ruled the country well.
③ He put a magic spell on them to make them like him.
④ He gave them money.

20. **Why did Morgana want Arthur's scabbard?**
① She thought it would look pretty in her house.
② She wanted to look after it for Arthur.
③ She guessed that it was worth a lot of money.
④ She knew that Arthur could not be killed while he had it.

21. Why did Arthur grow so tired in the battle? Choose two answers.

    ① He had been fighting for a long time.

    ② He was a very old man.

    ③ He could not move without his scabbard.

    ④ His armour was heavy.

22. How did Arthur kill Mordred?

    ① by stabbing him in the neck

    ② by throwing him onto the ground

    ③ by hitting him on the head with a sword

    ④ by smearing his face with dirt and blood

23. Where did Merlin take Arthur to die?

    ① Camelot

    ② Sir Ector's home

    ③ London

    ④ Avalon

※ Choose the wrong part of each sentence. (24~25)

24.
Sir Ector spent many hours to teach him.
　　　　①　　②　　　　③　　④

25.
Not everyone were pleased that a new High King had been found.
　　①　　　　②　　　　③　　　　　　　　　　　④

26. ① It made the dogs in the kennels barked in fear.
    ② It made the dogs in the kennels bark in fear.
    ③ It made the dogs in the kennels barks in fear.
    ④ It made the dogs in the kennels barking in fear.

27. ① You find a safe place him to grow and watch over him.
    ② Find a safe place to him to grow and watch over him.
    ③ Find a safe place for him to grow and watch over him.
    ④ Find a safe place for him grow and watch over him.

※ Choose the correct word or phrase for each blank. (28~30)

28.
> He grabbed hold of the sword and pulled as hard __________ he could.

① so   ② that
③ such   ④ as

29.
> It has magical qualities, of course, and __________ the scabbard.

① also have   ② so do
③ so does   ④ have too

30.
> Was it possible that he __________ some family, after all?

① has   ② have
③ does have   ④ did have

Memo

Memo 

Sarah J. Dodd
Sarah J. Dodd is an experienced primary school teacher who resides in the UK, but has also taught in Australia.
She has a PhD in Science and a certificate in Creative Writing. She has published four books for younger children
— 'An Angel Anyway' (Anyway Press) and the Little Angels' series (Lion Hudson plc). Her children's Bible will be
published in 2015. She is currently working on a novel for 9-12 year olds and another for young adults.

King Arthur

Retold by Sarah J. Dodd
Illustrated by Seongjin Kim

First Published in February 2015

Editorial Manager: Juyon Choi
Editors: Kyunghee Jang, Jiyeong Park
Designers: Eunhee Lee, Elim
Cover Designer: Eunhee Lee

Published and distributed by

Darakwon Bldg., 64-1 Jandari-ro, Mapo-gu, Seoul, Korea 121-894
Tel: 82-2-736-2031(ext. 250)   Fax: 82-2-736-2037
Homepage: www.ihappyhouse.co.kr
Publisher: Kyudo Chung

ISBN: 978-89-6653-173-8 18740 / 978-89-6653-156-1 18740(set)

[Components]
• 1 Audio CD (Recording Studio: Aram)
• Answer Keys & Korean Translation: Free download at www.ihappyhouse.co.kr